The Wingless Bird

Written by Detrick C. Greene
Dennis E. Pritchett Sr

The Wingless Bird Published in 2018
by It's A Love Thang Publishing Company

All rights reserved. No part of this publication may be reproduced, stored in a retrieval system or transmitted in any form by any means without the prior permission of the publishers and copyright owner.

ISBN: 9780692076996

Text © 2018 Detrick C. Greene
Illustration © 2018 Detrick C. Greene
Logo and design © 2018 Detrick C. Greene
Illustrations by Rajiv Kumar

Dedicated to my late Grandfather
Dennis E. "Sparkler-Man" Pritchett
wings earned in 2005

One sunny day in a forest called Greenwood, lived a new happy mom enjoying motherhood.

Birthed were five small birds.
"A cute little feathered gang".

Each of their lively personalities drove mom insane.

Gabby was sassy and Shelly was a mess.

Goldie was silly. She made everyone laugh within the nest.

Sam love crowns like queens and kings.

But, one tiny fellow had no wings.

Yet, Charlie loved to sing and joy to his family it would bring.

Soon began the time of year, where terrible storms were approaching near.

Oh, what a pitiful uncommon plight.

Charlie was alone from morning to night.

However, day-by-day, Charlie grew strong. Within the days Charlie missed his family, he would sing a song.

"Oh, we've seen lots of funny things".
But, Ha! Ha! Ha! "Look a bird without wings".

Charlie decided to prove to the others that he could fly.
"To him, my friend it was worth a try".

Suddenly, Charlie leaned out from his nest.
Landed on the ground. BAM! Flat on his chest.

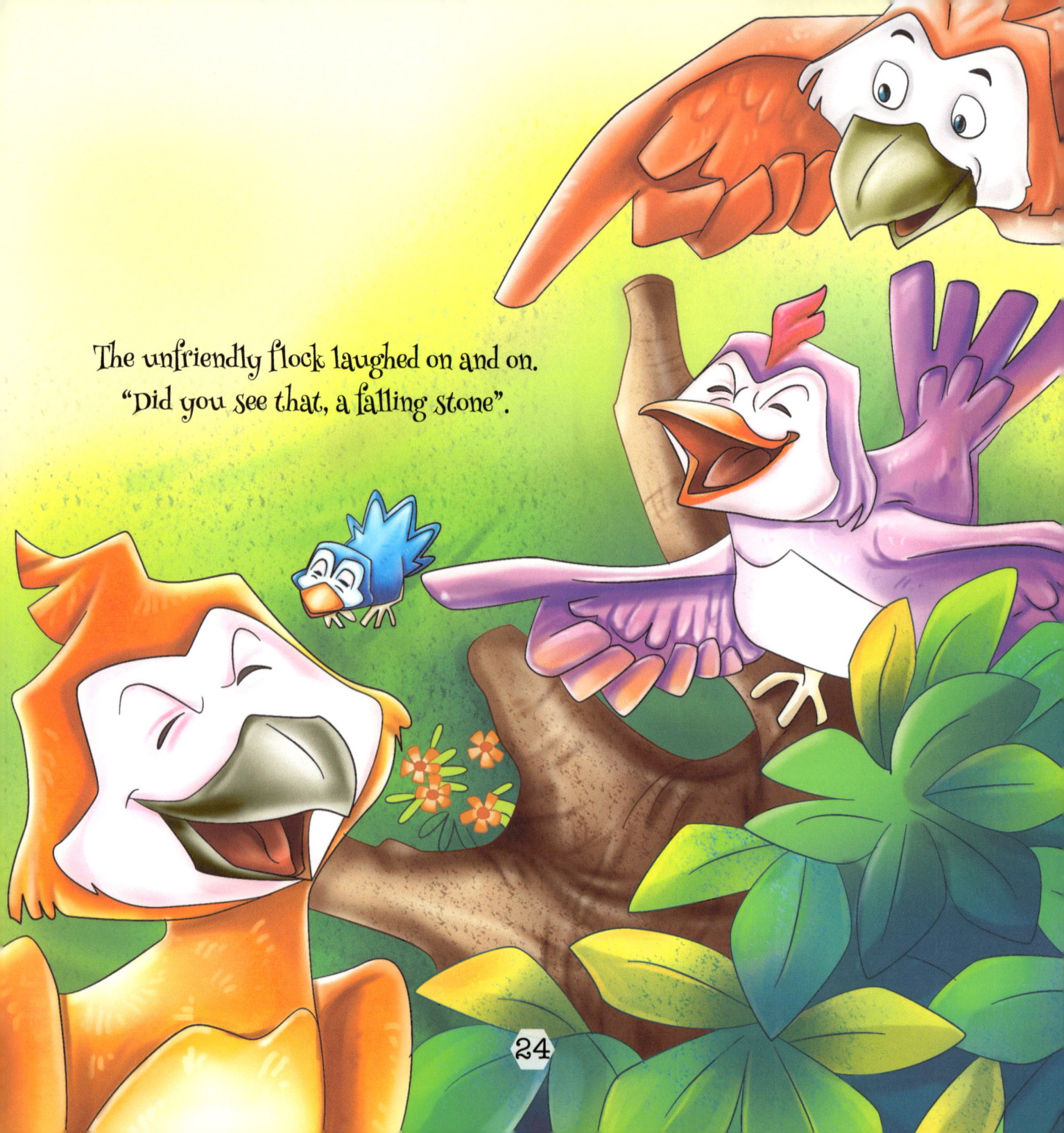

The unfriendly flock laughed on and on. "Did you see that, a falling stone".

Poor Charlie lay on the bare ground and his weeping was his only sound.

Quietly, Charlie fell asleep as he dreamed of a mountain extremely tall and steep.

There, Charlie stood at the very tip-top with big beautiful wings to flip and flop.

Immediately, Charlie awakes and recognizes that it was just a dream.
Charlie wanted to cry and he wanted to scream.

But, as time sailed swiftly by, Charlie repeated to himself, "I'm going to sing until I die".

With all of his might, Charlie sang as best he could, catching the attention of every animal in the forest of Greenwood.

Upon the branch Charlie stood, as he sang his songs loud and clear.
His songs were so good that they filled each animal's heart with love
laughter and cheer.

Unexpectedly, tears of joy took Charlie by surprise,
as he seen his family dancing together right before his eyes.

Now Charlie often flies in the skies above.

And just like Charlie, we too can fly, when we do the things we love.

The End!